Colossians
christ supreme

Linda Osborne

CONTENTS

Preface   1

1   Colossians 1   3

2   Colossians 2   15

3   Colossians 3   27

4   Colossians 4   39

    About the Author   50

PREFACE

❧

Written from a prison cell by the apostle Paul around A.D. 60, the letter to the Colossians is one of the most Christ-centered books in the Bible—the theme being the supremacy and all-sufficiency of Christ. Colossians and Ephesians have been called the twin epistles—written at the same time and with similar contents but with a twist: to the Ephesians Paul emphasized the *Church* of Christ, to the Colossians he emphasized the *Christ* of the Church.

Colosse was located approximately 100 miles east of Ephesus in the Lycus Valley in Asia Minor (in the general vicinity of the seven Asian churches of Revelation). Although at one time Colosse had thrived as a prominent city of commerce, by the time of Paul's writing its importance as a city was on the decline. It seems from this letter that Paul himself had not evangelized Colosse but that Epaphras was it founder. Colossians1:7, speaking of the gospel, says, "just as you learned it from Epaphras, our beloved fellow bond-servant, who is a faithful servant of Christ on our behalf." Epaphras had most likely been converted to Christ during Paul's three-year stay in Ephesus. From there it appears that Epaphras took the Good News he had received to areas like Colosse, Hierapolis, and Laodicea. At the time of Paul's writing it seems that Epaphras had traveled to Rome to visit with Paul or was himself in prison there (Philemon 23).

With the good news of the foundation and growth of the Colossian church, there also came concern. It seems that there was false teaching abounding and threatening the doctrinal purity of the church. From Greek philosophy to Jewish legalism to Oriental mysticism, the enemy was attempting to infiltrate and twist the pure and true doctrine of Christianity. Paul's letter was written in response to this disturbing news. His aim was to warn the church and to point them back to the truth. He had but one major answer to all of the erroneous teaching—Christ is supreme—therefore, faith in Christ is sufficient. If we could but grasp the enormity of this truth, it could change our lives forever! "For in Him all the fullness of Deity dwells in bodily form, and in Him you have been made complete, and He is the head over all rule and authority." Colossians 2:9-10

There is so much in this first chapter of Colossians; there is no way to adequately cover it in one lesson. It must be one of the fullest and most profound chapters in the entire Bible! Because we will only have the ability to scratch the surface in this lesson, please read and reread this chapter for yourself. It is full of treasure! And, as always, be sure to begin with prayer.

COLOSSIANS 1

✤

Day 1
Daily Facts
Read Colossians 1:1-14

1. How does Paul identify himself to the Colossian believers, and how does he define this position?

H.A. Ironside points out that, "Thirteen Epistles in the New Testament begin with the name 'Paul' … addressed either to churches among the Gentiles or to individual believers. Paul was the apostle to the Gentiles …"

    a. How does Paul, in Romans 11:13, concur with this statement?

Paul addresses himself to the believers in Colosse, beginning with his usual greeting of grace and peace and immediately expresses thankfulness to God for the Colossians because of what he has learned about them from Epaphras.

2. Verses 4-5 define their Christianity by way of three Christian virtues. According to Epaphras they had:

    ✤   faith in _____
    ✤   love for _____
    ✤   hope in _____

The Amplified Bible gives a wonderful expansion on the word faith, speaking of their faith in Christ (verse 4). It says, "The leaning of your entire human personality on Him in absolute trust and confidence in His power and wisdom and goodness."

   a. Using that as your standard for faith in Christ, how do you measure up? How might this definition make a difference in your perspective today, in the situation that is in front of you right now?

One commentator calls faith, love, and hope a trilogy of Christian virtues and says that they are a major theme for Christianity. Are they a major theme of your Christianity???

3. In verses 5-6, Paul speaks of the gospel as "the word of truth … which has come to you …" From verse 6, where else had the gospel message gone, and what was the result?

The Amplified Bible speaks of the gospel bearing fruit and growing "by its own inherent power."

   a. What does Romans 1:16 say about the gospel?

   b. What is the essence of the gospel? 1 Corinthians 15:3-4

   c. See if you can share the gospel message in a few sentences, using your own words.

4. In Colossians 1:13-14, Paul gives a glimpse of what took place for the Colossians through the death and resurrection of Christ.

✝ They were delivered from _____(v. 13)
✝ They were transferred to _____(v. 13)
✝ They were _____(v. 14)
✝ They were _____(v. 14)

a. Choose one of these truths of your salvation experience and share from your heart what it means to you.

b. If you have not yet made a commitment to Jesus as your personal Savior, which of these promises is most compelling to you and why?

Is there any reason to stay in the kingdom of darkness when redemption and forgiveness (deliverance from the guilt and doom of sin and introduction into a life of liberty) is available to you in Jesus Christ?

Let's look at Paul's prayer for the Colossians, found in verses 9-12. In verse 9, Paul says that from the day he heard of their faith he had not ceased to pray for them.

5. What did Paul ask the Father to do for his Colossian brothers and sisters? v. 9

Phillips translates this prayer: "We are asking God that you may be filled with such wisdom and that you may understand His purpose."

    a. What would be the practical outcome of the answer to Paul's prayer?

verse 10

verse 11

verse 12

Meditate on these verses. They are Paul's prayer for the Colossians—and they are God's heart for you! They are also a wonderful list of requests to make for those you love.

Stone of Remembrance:

"For I am not ashamed of the gospel, for it is the power of God for salvation to everyone who believes ..." Romans 1:16

Day 2
Daily Facts
Read Colossians 1:15-23

Paul's approach in bringing the Colossian's thinking back on track is significant. He doesn't begin by attacking the false doctrine they have been hearing—he begins by exalting Christ!

1. In verses 15-20, Paul tells us something we as Christians want to know—he tells us who Christ is. From each of the following verses, answer the question:

Who is He?

✠ 15a

✠ 15b

✠ 16-17

✠ 18a

✠ 18b

✠ 19

✠ 20

It has been said that these are some of the most important verses in the New Testament, establishing the deity of Jesus Christ. To help us in our understanding of what we have just been given, we will look at other verses in the Bible confirming these key truths.

✠ He is the image of the invisible God

John 14:9

Hebrews 1:3a

✠ He is the firstborn of all creation

Psalm 89:27

Revelation 1:17b

✠ He is the creator

John 1:3

Hebrews 1:2

✠ He is the head of the body

Ephesians 1:22-23

Ephesians 5:23

✠ He is the beginning, the firstborn from among the dead

Romans 1:4

1 Corinthians 15:20

✠ He is the fullness of God

Colossians 2:9

Hebrews 1:8

✠ He is the reconciler

Romans 5:10-11

2 Corinthians 5:18-19

✠ Have you gained any new insight into the character of Christ from these verses? Share one aspect of your renewed understanding of who Christ is.

2. In Colossians 1:21-23, Paul again brings us back to the essence of the gospel message. Answer the following questions from a personal point of view:

   a. Before reconciliation to Christ, what was your state? v. 21

   b. Because of your reconciliation to Christ, what is now your state before God? v. 22

   c. How does 2 Corinthians 5:21 define this incredible miracle?

   d. With your personal understanding of the gospel message, explain this miracle in your own words.

If you have not yet received Jesus Christ as your personal Savior, is there any reason why you shouldn't right now? Romans 5:6 says, "For while we were still helpless, at the right time Christ died for the ungodly." If you are still helpless—still held captive by your sin—simply turn to Christ and ask Him to come into your life and save you from the bondage and penalty of your sin. He is just waiting to hear from you!

Review this week's memory verse.

Day 3
Daily Facts
Read Colossians 1:24-29

Before Paul even began to minister—in fact at the very onset of his Christian experience, Jesus Christ made the statement of Paul, "I will show him how much he must suffer for My name's sake." Paul's ministry, much like his Savior's, was linked from the beginning to suffering. We must remember from where he wrote this letter.

1. For whose sake did Paul say he suffered in verse 24?

    a. Paul had never met these particular believers, how could he say he suffered for their sake? See 2 Corinthians 11:28-29 for your answer.

Although Paul was specifically speaking to the Colossians, he speaks here of doing his share on behalf of Christ's body—the Church.

    b. What did he say his personal suffering was accomplishing in regard to the body of Christ? v. 24b

Verse 24 has been difficult for many to understand. Paul was in no way speaking of sharing in Christ's saving sacrifice but rather in the work of perfecting those who are saved. As a minister to the body of Christ, Paul placed himself in a position to be hated by those who hated Christ.

2. 2 Timothy 2:8-9 describes one aspect of Paul's suffering for the gospel. What does it say?

a. 2 Timothy 2:10 reveals why Paul is willing to endure such hardship. For what reason does he endure these things?

3. Paul was serious about his calling. From Colossians 1:25:

a. Who called him to ministry?

b. For whose benefit did he minister?

c. What was his ministry?

4. Paul was excited about his message. From verse 26:

a. How does Paul describe the message he has to give?

b. According to verse 27, what is the mystery that has now been revealed?

Although this revelation concerns all believers, it is especially significant to the Gentiles, who up until this point had been excluded from the promises reserved for the Jews.

5. What does Ephesians 3:6 say about this?

a. How does Ephesians 2:12-14 describe what Christ has made possible for the Gentile?

b. What does Galatians 3:28 add to this?

Previously God's special revelation was to the Jew alone. Now Paul speaks to the Gentiles of the riches of the glory of this mystery, which is "Christ in you, the hope of glory"! Previous to the death and resurrection of Christ, in the Jewish economy, the Gentile had no hope. Now he had the hope of glory!!! Now, because of the saving work of Christ, all men—even those who were Gentiles—could be saved and indwelt by Christ.

6. From verses 28-29, what were the three aspects of Paul's ministry?

   a. What was his goal for every believer?

   b. Although Paul personally labored, even striving to fulfill the purpose for which he was called, whose power did Paul say was working within him?

"For this I labor [unto weariness], striving with all the superhuman energy which He so mightily enkindles and works within me."
v. 29 Amplified Bible

   c. From where did Paul get this mighty power? Acts 1:8

Paul did his part—he proclaimed, he admonished, and he taught. God did His part by the mighty working of the Holy Spirit—He empowered Paul to fulfill his ministry. If you feel the need for more strength or power from the Lord to enable you to live the Christian life and to be useful to the Lord in ministering to others, it is available to you for the asking!

"If you then being evil, know how to give good gifts to your children, how much more shall your heavenly Father give the Holy Spirit to those who ask Him?" Luke 11:13

Review this week's memory verse.

Day 4
Overview of Colossians 1

Today we will be looking at the passage we have studied this week as a whole. The goal is to find the main lessons the Lord has for us from this chapter. Don't worry about being clever or profound—just do your best!

Find the Facts ...

1. See if you can state the *content* of this week's passage in a couple of sentences. (Who is speaking, what is taking place, what is the main subject?)

Look for the Heart ...

2. What do you think is the main *lesson* of this chapter? (What spiritual truths are taught here? Look for a command, a word of exhortation, a promise, etc.)

Hear Him Speak...

3. Look for a *personal application* from the content of this chapter. It should come from the lesson you got from the chapter (question 2). How will you apply the lesson to yourself?

4. Was there a particular verse that ministered to you this week? What was it and how did it minister to you?

5. Write out your stone of remembrance *from memory*!

COLOSSIANS 2

⚜

Day 1
Daily Facts
Read Colossians 2:1-7

1. On whose behalf does Paul say he struggles in Colossians 2:1?

   a. What is one form or manner that Paul's struggle for the church most likely manifested itself? See Colossians 1:3, 9 and 4:12

The word for struggle in verse 1 is *agon*, from which we get our word agony. Does that give you a sense of Paul's great burden for these churches that he has never even seen?

   b. Did Paul love these people personally? Who is it that Paul loves?

The type of prayer that Paul would have made on behalf of these believers is known as intercessory prayer. The dictionary definition of intercede is "to plead or petition in behalf of another; to come between parties in a dispute; to mediate." Literally, it means to pass or go between, and on a spiritual level it speaks of taking the place of another person before God and pleading on their behalf.

15

Norman P. Grubb says of intercessory prayer: "There are three things to be seen in an intercessor which are not necessarily found in ordinary prayer: identification, agony and authority ... Intercession so identifies the intercessor with the sufferer that it gives him a prevailing place with God."

Paul had never met the Colossians or the Laodiceans, but he so identified with their needs in Christ that we might assume it gave him a prevailing place with God on their behalf!

2.   According to the following verses, who intercedes for us?

Romans 8:26-27

Romans 8:34 and Hebrews 7:25

a. What does it do for your faith to know that Christ *always lives to make intercession for you*?

b. According to 1 Timothy 2:1-2, for whom are we to intercede?

c. Read James 5:13-16 on the subject of prayer. Fill in the last sentence with your name: "The effective prayer of _____ can accomplish much!"

3. In verse 2, Paul specifically states that over which he struggles for the Colossians. What were his deep desires for these people?

a. What is the mystery that Paul speaks of in verse 2b?

16

   b. Describe Him from verse 3.

We must remember here that Paul is writing this letter to the Colossians to refute the false teaching that they are receiving. Here he sets the foundation that Christ is sufficient—in Him are hidden all the treasures of wisdom and knowledge! If you have Christ, you need not look elsewhere for answers to life: "The fear of the Lord is the beginning of wisdom, and the knowledge of the Holy One is understanding." Proverbs 9:10

4. Verse 6 says, "As you therefore have received Christ Jesus the Lord, so walk in Him." How did you receive Jesus Christ?

   a. How does Romans 10:9-10 say that a person is saved?

   b. In a word or two, what would you say our part of salvation is?

5. What do you think it means to *walk in the Lord*? (You may see 1 John 2:6)

   a. If you received Jesus as Lord and Savior *by faith*, how then will you be enabled to walk in Him? 2 Corinthians 5:7 What do you think this means?

6. Share some practical ways you can let your roots grow down into Christ so that you will grow strong and vigorous in the truth you have been taught (v. 7).

Stone of Remembrance:

"It was for freedom that Christ set us free; therefore keep standing firm and do not be subject again to a yoke of slavery." Galatians 5:1

Day 2
Daily Facts
Read Colossians 2: 8-15

1. In verses 8-10, Paul refutes worldly philosophy. What strong word of warning does Paul speak to the Colossians (and to us today, as well)? v. 8

   a. The word philosophy means "to love wisdom." Certainly Paul loved wisdom as much as anyone, what kind of wisdom was he opposed to according to verse 8?

   b. James 3:14-16 speaks of "worldly wisdom;" what picture does it paint?

   c. What kind of wisdom would Paul have the Colossians cling to (v 8b)? See why from verse 3.

   d. What does James 3:17 teaches us about "the wisdom from above"?

"See to it that no one takes you captive" is a strong statement. The word captive is from a Greek word meaning "to carry off as booty." It means essentially "to kidnap." See to it that no one *kidnaps* you away from the truth found only in Christ.

2.   According to Paul's words in Colossians 1:13:

   a.   From what had they been delivered?

   b.   To what had they been transferred?

   c.   What does Paul say in Galatians 5:1 that gives the spirit of his words here?

3.   In Colossians 2:9-10, Paul gives us a picture of the person of Christ:

   a.   How does Paul portray Christ? v. 9

   b.   How does Paul portray the believer in Christ? v. 10

   c.   If Christ is the head over all rule and authority (2:10b), the Creator of all mankind (1:16) and Sustainer of all things (1:17), is there any reason to look to mankind for life's answers? Share.

Paul has spoken a warning against the emptiness of the worldly philosophy being pushed on the Colossians by false teachers. Now, in verses 11-12, he begins to speak against legalism, which also held the potential of taking away their freedom in Christ. His word to the Colossians is, don't be *intimidated by legalism.*

Circumcision was an Old Testament rite given by God to Israel to identify them as belonging to Him. The cutting away of the flesh symbolized cutting off the old life of sin, purifying one's heart, and dedicating oneself to God.

Remember that in speaking to the Colossians, Paul was primarily speaking to Gentiles who had not entered into the covenant of God by physical circumcision, and yet we see Paul speak of them as being circumcised.

4.   How were they circumcised according to verse 11?

The key thought in this verse is, "In Him."

    a.   What else had taken place for these believers in Christ? v. 12

Obviously, the Colossians had not been physically buried with Christ or raised with Christ from the dead. Paul is speaking in these verses of spiritual realities that took place when they identified with Christ through faith. Because of their spiritual identification with Christ, the Colossian believers did not need to go through the physical act of circumcision in order to be saved.

    b.   These are difficult concepts to understand. To help us with all of these difficult spiritual truths, what simple truth does 2 Corinthians 5:17 tell us?

    c.   To sum up Paul's warning against the legalists who would put them back under the Jewish law, what does 1 Corinthians 7:18-20 say?

5. Verses 13-15 give us a vivid picture of what happened for us at the cross of Christ.

From verses 13-14:
- ✢ What condition were we in?
- ✢ What did He make us?
- ✢ Of what did He forgive us?
- ✢ What did He cancel for us?
- ✢ How did He do this?

Romans 3:23 says: "For all have sinned and fall short of the glory of God." Romans 6:23 says: "For the wages of sin is death." This is the certificate of debt that was against us. We have sinned, therefore we are in debt to God—and the wages of sin is death. But God took that certificate of our debt and nailed it to the cross of His dear Son, and through the death of Jesus, our debt was paid.

From verse 15:

- ✢ Who did He disarm?
- ✢ What did He do to them?
- ✢ Who triumphed at the cross?

A most amazing thing happened at the cross—the place of the degradation and humiliation of Jesus Christ. It looked as if Satan's plan to be rid of Jesus had prevailed, but in reality, God's plan to redeem the world through the death of His Son was fulfilled! Satan's evil plan was turned into a victory for God, His Son, and all of mankind!

Review this week's memory verse.

Day 3
Daily Facts
Read Colossians 2:16-23

1. Since we are alive in Christ, our debt has been forgiven—even canceled out forever in Christ—and we are free, no longer subject to slavery. Therefore, what does Paul say in verse 16?

Again, Paul speaks of legalism. The legalistic believer thinks he has to do something to earn credit with God. Paul has just shown that it was all done for him or her in Christ.

    a. What kinds of things might a person do to attempt to earn credit with God?

    b. Do you ever feel the need to do such things? Has the teaching of Colossians 2 helped you to understand that you don't need to do anything but believe and look to Christ? Share your thoughts.

The thing to note here is that it doesn't matter whether or not they eat or drink or what day they celebrate—it is that no one is to act as their judge in these things. In Christ they are free. The Jewish dietary laws, festivals, and sacrifices were all things that pointed to Christ—they were a shadow of what was to come—the substance is found in Christ.

Verses 18-19 speak of mysticism. John MacArthur says that, "Mysticism may be defined as the pursuit of a deeper or higher religious experience … It looks for truth internally, weighing feelings, intuition and other internal sensations …" Again—not trusting in Christ alone—thinking there is more for the special few!

Notice how strong Paul's warnings are: "See to it that no one takes you captive" (v. 8), "Therefore, let no one act as your judge" (v. 16). "Let no one keep defrauding you of your prize" (v. 18).

2. What were some of the mystic's rules for spirituality according to verse 18?

    a. How does Paul diagnose the truth of the situation in verse 18b?

Like the legalists, the mystics were looking to themselves for spiritual success rather than to Christ. In verse 19, Paul says they were not holding fast to the Head, which is Christ.

3. From this verse, how important is it to be attached to the Head?

    a. What kind of growth is there for the one who is attached and supplied by the Head? v. 19b

    b. See if you can apply the truth of John 15:4-5 to the concept we have here.

MacArthur says, "We, like the Colossians, must not be intimidated by those who would make something other than knowing Christ through His word a requisite for spiritual maturity."

In verses 20-23, Paul speaks of asceticism. An ascetic is one who lives a life of self-denial in order to gain spirituality. This was part of the error of the Colossian false teachers—attempting to gain righteousness through self-denial or harsh treatment of the body. Notice Paul's words in verse 23: "These are matters which have ... the appearance of wisdom, in self-made religion and self-abasement and severe treatment of the body ..."

4. Does this self-religion have the power to change the heart? v. 23b

    a. What is the word of Jesus pertaining to righteous (Spirit-led) self-denial? Matthew 16:24

    b. See if you can explain why it would be easier (not better or more righteous but easier) to follow a list of man-made rules—even to the point of denying yourself food or comfort, than to take up your cross and follow Jesus.

Review this week's memory verse.

Day 4
Overview of Colossians 2

Today we will be looking at the passage we have studied this week as a whole. The goal is to find the main lessons the Lord has for us from this chapter. Don't worry about being clever or profound—just do your best!

Find the Facts ...

1. See if you can state the *content* of this week's passage in a couple of sentences. (Who is speaking, what is taking place, what is the main subject?)

Look for the Heart ...

2. What do you think is the main *lesson* of this chapter? (What spiritual truths are taught here? Look for a command, a word of exhortation, a promise, etc.)

Hear Him Speak ...

3. Look for a *personal application* from the content of this chapter. It should come from the lesson you got from the chapter (question 2). How will you apply the lesson to yourself?

4. Was there a particular verse that ministered to you this week? What was it and how did it minister to you?

5. Write out your stone of remembrance *from memory*!

COLOSSIANS 3

❖

Day 1
Daily Facts
Read Colossians 3:1-4

The first half of Paul's letter to the Colossians deals with doctrine; the second half deals with duty. The first half deals with the supremacy of Christ, the second with the submission of the Christian. And in the chapter we will look at this week, the first four verses deal with position (the believer's position in Christ), and the rest of the chapter deals with practice (the practice of the believer in Christ).

The first word in verse 1 in many translations is the word *if*. The word should really be translated *since* or *because*. Because you have been raised up with Christ ...

1.   What should you do? (In a few words):

     verse 1

     verse 2

     a.   What (actually, Who) is above, according to verse 1?

     b.   Where are you (positionally, not physically)? v. 1a

2. We saw this truth presented in Colossians 2:12. Reread this verse and share what we learned there about our position in Christ.

   a. Romans 6:5 teaches us this same concept. What does it say?

Obviously, you are still physically *alive on planet earth*. But positionally, you are *seated in the heavenlies with Christ*—so sure is your salvation! It is finished!

Galatians 2:20 is one of the most profound verses—sharing this same eternal and amazing truth. In the Amplified Bible, it is translated in this manner: "I have been crucified with Christ [in Him I have shared His crucifixion]; it is no longer I who live, but Christ (the Messiah) lives in me; and the life I now live in the body I live by faith in (by adherence to and reliance on and complete trust in) the Son of God, who loved me and gave Himself up for me."

3. The word *seek* in verse 1(keep seeking the things above), has the meaning of "striving for;" and the word *set* in verse 2 (set your mind on the things above), has the meaning of "concentrating on." What are some ways you can strive for and concentrate on the things above?

   a. How do the following verses help us with these thoughts?

   Matthew 6:33

   Romans 12:2

2 Corinthians 4:18

Philippians 4:8

4. Why is it that we should set our hearts and minds on the things above? v. 3

Here again, we see that, although we are physically here, God sees us co-crucified and co-raised with Jesus Christ. You and I are hidden in Jesus Christ. It is a completed work. Nothing can disturb the union and position that you have in Christ.

  a. Romans 8:31-39 gives us a picture of the complete safety and security there is for the one who is "in Christ." Read these wonderful verses and pick out a verse or two that most encourages you today.

5. Because our life is hidden with Christ in God, what is the future hope of every believer in Christ? Colossians 3:4

  a. 1 Thessalonians 4:16-17 describes the moment when the Lord will come and gather His children from this world to be with Him forever. What is the message of this passage?

  b. Using Philippians 3:21, what exactly will Jesus do for us on that day?

c. Finally, what does 1 John 3:2 say about that time when we are with Christ?

Stone of Remembrance:

"I have been crucified with Christ; and it is no longer I who live, but Christ lives in me; and the life which I now live in the flesh I live by faith in the Son of God, who loved me, and delivered Himself up for me." Galatians 2:20

Day 2
Daily Facts

Read Colossians 3:5-17

Verses 1-4 set the stage for what is to follow. Verse 5 begins with the word *therefore*. Because of the believer's death with Christ, he must regard himself as dead to the old sins and put them off. Because of the believer's resurrection with Christ, he must regard himself as alive to righteousness and put on the new life with its qualities.

In verses 5-9, Paul gives us a list of the sorts of things that the Christian is to put off.

1. List the first five personal sins from verse 5.

   a. In what way does Paul further define the sin of greed?

It almost seems as if the first four sins go hand in hand and that the final one, greed, is of another nature. But is it?

   b. See if you can define what *greed* or *covetousness* is.

c. How might the sin of greed be the basis for the other sins mentioned here?

2. How are we to see ourselves in regard to these sins? v. 5a

   a. Why does Paul say we are to regard ourselves this way? v. 6-7

   b. How does Ephesians 2:1-7 motivate you to lay aside (or put off) these sins of your former life?

3. From Colossians 3:8-9 list the next six sins Paul asks us to put off. (These sins are not so much personal as they are social.)

   a. Personal: (not to be shared in group) Are you struggling today with any of the sins Paul has listed in these verses? If you are, get before the Lord right now in prayer, and ask Him first to forgive you for your sin and then to give you the power of His Holy Spirit to put off these sins that Christ died for.

John MacArthur says, "How can we be victorious in our struggle against sin? First by starving it. Do not feed anger or resentment. Do not cater to sexual lust or covetousness. Second by crowding it out with positive graces …" and he quotes Philippians 4:8 and Colossians 3:16.

Putting off the old, they are now to put on the new. In verses 12-14, Paul gives us a list of those things that should characterize the Christian, who is a new creature in Christ (2 Corinthians 5:17), chosen of God, holy and beloved (Colossians 3:12). H.A. Ironside looks at these virtues as the clothing of the Christian and calls them the garments of glory!

4. Beginning with verse 12, what kind of a heart are we to put on?

   a. Who is our example in each of these Christian graces? (Matthew 11:29)

   b. What two things are we to do for each other? v. 13 Why?

   c. How does verse 14 tie it all together? (Ironside says of this verse, "Here we have the belt that holds all our new garments in place.")

   d. How do we get this love? Romans 5:5

5. In verses 15-17, Paul gives 3 priorities for this new life in Christ. What are they?

   ✦   verse 15

   a. How might the peace of God ruling in your heart help you to know if you are walking according to the new life in Christ or the old life of sin?

✝ verse 16

b. What does Psalm 119:11 say about our need for God's word?

Notice in verse 16 we have the Word and we have worship. The two go hand in hand, ministering to the body of Christ.

✝ verse 17

c. How would it make a difference in your actions and words if everything you did was done in the name of Jesus Christ?

Notice that in each of these last three verses there is a call to thankfulness. Do you have a thankful heart? It will truly make all the difference as you endeavor to be clothed with the characteristics of Christ.

Review this week's memory verse.

Day 3
Daily Facts
Read Colossians 3:18-25

The first and most important relationships we will look at are in regard to the home. Genesis 2:18-25 gives us the beginning of the marriage relationship.

1. From these Genesis verses:

a. Why did God make the woman? v. 18

b. How did He make her? v. 21-22

c. What was Adam's perception of Eve? v. 23

d. What did they become? v. 24b

2. How does 1 Corinthians 11:8-9 give us an understanding of God's purpose for the woman?

In this day of feministic teaching and worldly thinking this might come as a great surprise. But it is God's Word, and it will only be when we understand and have a holy regard for His word that our relationships will become pure and peaceful and Christ-like.

a. What word to the wife does Paul speak in Colossians 3:18?

The Amplified version of 1 Peter 3:1-2 gives us the best understanding of how we are to behave as wives: "In like manner, you married women, be submissive to your own husbands [subordinate yourselves as being secondary to and dependent on them, and adapt yourselves to them], so that even if any do not obey the Word [of God], they may be won over not by discussion but by the [godly] lives of their wives. When they observe the pure and modest way in which you conduct yourselves, together with your reverence [for your husband; you are to feel for him all that reverence includes: to respect, defer to, revere him—to honor, esteem, appreciate, prize, and, in the human sense, to adore him, that is, to admire, praise, be devoted to, deeply love, and enjoy your husband]."

✝ If you are married, is there anything in these verses that you need to change in your relationship with your husband?

✝ If you want to be married someday, is there anything here that you might need to adjust your thinking on before you become a wife?

3. What is Paul's command to the husband? v.19

   a. Even as 1 Peter has a strong word for the wife, it has a word to the husband as well. From 1 Peter 3:7, how is the husband to live with his wife, and what will happen if he does not? (v. 7b)

   b. What example does Paul give the husband for loving his wife? Ephesians 5:25

   c. As the wife submits herself to her husband with love and respect, and the husband loves his wife in a sacrificial way, what do you think will happen in the marriage?

If you are struggling in your marriage today, you don't have to wait until your husband becomes what he is called to be—begin today to do your part: defer to him, respect him, love him. You will be amazed at the changes you will see in your marriage!

4. The next important relationship that Paul speaks about is the relationship of parents and children. What does he say to the children? v. 20

    a. Do you think the obligation to honor your parents ends when you move out on your own? See Exodus 20:12

    b. What does he say to the parents? v. 21

    c. Raising children is a difficult task—one that takes great patience and maturity. If you are a parent today, what changes might you need to make in the way you relate to your child in order not to provoke him or cause him to lose heart?

The final relationship in our passage today is the relationship between slaves and masters. The best example we have of this today is the relationship of employer and employee.

5. How is the employee to serve their employer? v. 22

    a. What perspective would make all the difference for the one called on to serve or work for another in this way? v. 23-24

The final thought in verse 25 really sums it all up—each one will receive the reward of his or her actions. This, again, applies to every relationship.

If you are in a difficult relationship today, whether with your spouse, parent, child or employer—you do what you have been commanded by the Lord, knowing that it is the Lord you serve and from Him you will receive your reward, and leave the rest with Him.

Review this week's memory verse.

Day 4
Overview of Colossians 3

Today we will be looking at the passage we have studied this week as a whole. The goal is to find the main lessons the Lord has for us from this chapter. Don't worry about being clever or profound—just do your best!

Find the Facts ...

1. See if you can state the *content* of this week's passage in a couple of sentences. (Who is speaking, what is taking place, what is the main subject?)

Look for the Heart ...

2. What do you think is the main *lesson* of this chapter? (What spiritual truths are taught here? Look for a command, a word of exhortation, a promise, etc.)

Hear Him Speak ...

3. Look for a *personal application* from the content of this chapter. It should come from the lesson you got from the chapter (question 2). How will you apply the lesson to yourself?

4. Was there a particular verse that ministered to you this week? What was it and how did it minister to you?

5. Write out your stone of remembrance *from memory*!

COLOSSIANS 4

❦

Day 1
Daily Facts

Read Colossians 4:1-6 (concentrating on verses 1-2)

The first verse in Colossians 4 is really Paul's final thought regarding the believer's attitude toward relationships, which he began in Colossians 3:18.

1. What does Paul say to masters?

   a. What did we learn about all men who came to believe in Christ? 2 Corinthians 5:17

   b. How does Colossians 3:11 show that, as new creatures in Christ, the slave and the master are equal?

   c. What would be the rule in regard to relationships for all who are now in Christ? Matthew 7:12

2. In verse 2, Paul gives us three directions concerning prayer. What are they?

We will look at the first of these today.

    a. What does it mean to be "devoted" to something? Think about how you act in regard to the things you are devoted to or maybe we could say are *passionate* about.

3. 1 Thessalonians 5:17 gives us what seems to be an extreme word on the subject of praying—what does it say?

    a. What do you think this means?

This is not something that happens automatically when we are born-again, but the more we devote ourselves to God and prayer, the more we become conscious of God in every aspect of our life and find ourselves unconsciously praying without ceasing.

    b. Are you devoted to prayer? In what way does this devotion manifest itself in your life?

    c. If you are not devoted to prayer, what might you do to make this important spiritual discipline a priority in your life?

If a Christian is not devoted to prayer, it is very likely because he does not yet have a true sense of the power there is in prayer.

4. This is a very long list of verses—but one that really gives us a sense of not only the importance of prayer but the blessedness—even the wonder—of prayer. Share a few words from the heart of each one:

✝ 2 Chronicles 7:14

✝ Psalm 34:17

✝ Psalm 91:15

✝ Isaiah 65:24

✝ Matthew 7:7-8

✝ Mark 11:24

✝ Luke 18:1

✝ Romans 8:26

✝ Ephesians 3:20

✝ Hebrews 4:16

✝ James 4:2b

a. After looking at these verses, do you have a new appreciation of the power and the privilege of prayer?

Stone of Remembrance:

"Lord teach us to pray ..." Luke 11:1

Day 2
Daily Facts
Read Colossians 4:2-6

1. Besides the call to devote ourselves to prayer, Paul gives 2 other directives for prayer in verse 2. What are they?

    a. What would you say it means to keep alert in prayer? What is it like not to be alert in prayer—what kind of prayers would you pray if you were not alert in prayer?

Paul's exhortation to keep alert in prayer might also be a warning against spiritual drowsiness, as well as a call to alertness in waiting and watching for the Lord's return.

2. What do these verses say on this subject?

    Matthew 24:42

    1 Corinthians 16:13

    1 Thessalonians 5:6

    a. Do you think of yourself as an alert and awake Christian, not only in your prayers, but also in your attitude towards the Lord and His coming? Do you realize that the Lord's coming is at hand? Read 1 Peter 4:7 and share the exhortation given there.

b. Romans 13:11-12 is wonderful on this point. Evaluate your state of awareness of the nearness of the Lord. Are you living as if He could return any day? Are you awake? How might prayer make a difference in your life on this point? Are there some changes in your lifestyle you want to make?

The third factor in Paul's exhortation is thankfulness.

3. Look at Philippians 4:6—the antidote to anxiety. What are the ingredients of the antidote?

a. Make a list of some of the things we communicate to God when we pray with thanksgiving.

b. Do you have a thankful heart? This is such an important message of Colossians! Why do you think it's so important that we be thankful?

Paul has spoken of his prayers for them (1:3, 9-12); he has taught them the importance of being prayerful (4:2), and now he asks them to pray for him!

4. What specific prayer requests does Paul make in verses 3-4?

a. Do you pray for your pastor? Does this verse help you to see particular ways you can pray for him? What else might you pray for your pastor?

One of the wonderful things about prayer is that it makes us a part of the ministry in a way we might never be otherwise. We can pray for our pastors, evangelists and missionaries and share in the rewards of their labors!

Paul gives two final words of exhortation in his letter to the Colossian church, both that will make a difference in our effect upon the world.

5. How are we to conduct ourselves toward outsiders (non-Christians) according to verse 5?

    a. What are some ways that Christians can conduct themselves unwisely toward non-Christians—hindering rather than helping the cause of Christ?

    b. Are you making the most of your opportunities with those God has brought into your path? What are some of the different ways you can witness to your unbelieving friends, family, neighbors, and co-workers?

    c. Read Paul's words in 1 Corinthians 9:19-23. What do you think Paul is saying here?

6. How are we to speak, in order to make a difference in our world? v. 6

a. 1 Peter 3:15 hits the nail on the head when it comes to using our mouths to bring blessing to others and glory to God. What do you learn from this verse?

b. What difference would it make if you made Colossians 4:6 along with Ephesians 4:29 your standard for speaking?

Review this week's memory verse.

Day 3
Daily Facts
Read Colossians 4:7-18

1. Before we begin to look over this great list of Paul's helpers and companions, let's look at 1 Corinthians 12:12-31. In a sentence or two:

    a. What is the gist of verses 12-20? (See especially v. 12, 14, and 20.)

    b. What is the gist of verses 21-26?

    c. What is the gist of verses 27-31?

Although the apostle Paul was a great man with a great message—he did not work alone. All through his ministry, Paul was given help by other members of the body of Christ—each one having his own ministry and gifts. John MacArthur says of this portion of Scripture that, "… [Paul] encloses with his letter a verbal group photograph."

2. From each of the following verses in Colossians 4, name the face in the photograph and tell what you learn about him. (For those who want to dig deeper, additional verses are given in parenthesis for you to gain a better understanding of the part each one played in the ministry of Paul. You may even want to add any other information you know about these servants of God.)

    ✝ verses 7-8 (Acts 20:4; Ephesians 6:21-22 and 2 Timothy 4:12; Titus 3:12)

    ✝ verse 9 (Philemon 10-18)

    ✝ verse 10a (Acts 19:29, 20:4, 27:2; Philemon 24)

    ✝ verse 10b (Acts 12:25, 13:13, 15:37-40; Philemon 24; 2 Timothy 4:11)

    ✝ verse 11a

✦ verse 12-13 (Colossians 1:7)

✦ verse 14a (Philemon 24; 2 Timothy 4:11)

✦ verse 14b (Philemon 24; 2 Timothy 4:10)

Paul closes his letter with his greetings to the brethren in Colosse.

3.   Who does Paul want to specifically greet? v. 15

    a.   What does he ask the Colossians to do for him? v. 16

Many think the letter Paul mentions as coming from Laodicea is in fact the letter to the Ephesians. It seems that these letters would be read to the local congregations and then passed on to churches nearby. You see, they only had one copy of the beloved letter. They didn't have a Bible (or several) in each individual home! That should give us an extremely thankful heart when we realize that on any given day, at any time we can turn to one of Paul's letters, take in the instruction, exhortation, and blessed truths that he has written on behalf of the church!

Paul never lets an opportunity pass to minister and encourage his brethren. At the final moments of his letter, he remembers Archippus and sends this exhortation:

Take heed to your ministry—fulfill it! What an encouraging word this is to all who have been given a ministry in the Lord—let us fulfill it!

4.   What final request does Paul make of the Colossians? v. 18

   a.   What final blessing does he give?

5.   In what way has God met you in Paul's letter to the Colossians? Is there anything you saw for the first time? Anything you saw in a fresh and more accurate way? How did God bless you through this magnificent Christ-centered letter?

Review this week's memory verse.

Day 4
Overview of Colossians 4

Today we will be looking at the passage we have studied this week as a whole. The goal is to find the main lessons the Lord has for us from this chapter. Don't worry about being clever or profound—just do your best!

Find the Facts…

1.   See if you can state the *content* of this week's passage in a couple of sentences. (Who is speaking, what is taking place, what is the main subject?)

Look for the Heart ...

2. What do you think is the main *lesson* of this chapter? (What spiritual truths are taught here? Look for a command, a word of exhortation, a promise, etc.)

Hear Him Speak ...

3. Look for a *personal application* from the content of this chapter. It should come from the lesson you got from the chapter (question 2). How will you apply the lesson to yourself?

4. Was there a particular verse that ministered to you this week? What was it and how did it minister to you?

5. Write out your stone of remembrance *from memory*!

ABOUT THE AUTHOR

❖

Linda has dedicated her life to serving the Lord as a teacher, writer, and speaker. While teaching the Word of God, training leaders, and speaking at retreats and other women's ministry functions, she has also written curriculum for over 20 books of the Bible.

If you would be interested in having more information about her ministry, please visit her blog at www.lindaoborne.wordpress.com, or email her at myutmost1@aol.com.

www.ingramcontent.com/pod-product-compliance
Lightning Source LLC
Chambersburg PA
CBHW060618030426
42337CB00018B/3112